HENRY MOORE AT THE BRITISH MUSEUM

HENRY MOORE AT THE BRITISH MUSEUM

BY HENRY MOORE

Photographs by David Finn

Published for the Trustees of the British Museum
by British Museum Publications Ltd

Acknowledgments

I paid seven or eight private visits to the British Museum in the making of this book and as at the time I had injured my back, I decided to use a wheelchair. To go round the galleries when they are empty of people, in a wheelchair, with no physical effort to oneself, I recommend to everybody as the perfect way to visit a museum. I am very grateful to my fellow Yorkshireman Dr D. M. Wilson, Director, to his assistant Miss Marjorie Caygill and to the security warders, for making these visits possible.

The Keeper of each department was available to accompany me and to give me his expert knowledge when needed – and also, unlike the ordinary visitor, I was privileged actually to handle some of the smaller works, objects I had admired on my first visits to the British Museum as a student sixty years ago. For all this pleasure, therefore, I would like to thank Mr B. F. Cook, Keeper of Greek and Roman Antiquities, Mr T. G. H. James, Keeper of Egyptian Antiquities and Mr M. D. McLeod, Keeper of Ethnography, The Museum of Mankind.

And of course to David Finn go my warm thanks for the immense amount of time and trouble he has taken with the photography.

H.M.

British Library Cataloguing in Publication Data
Moore, Henry, *1898–*
    Henry Moore at the British Museum
    1. Sculpture
    I. Title   II. Finn, David
    730'.9   NB60

ISBN 0-7141-2010-3

Published by British Museum Publications Ltd,
46 Bloomsbury Street, London, WC1B 3QQ

Designed by James Shurmer

Set in Monophoto Bembo and printed in Great Britain by
W. S. Cowell Ltd, Ipswich

Frontispiece Henry Moore outside the British Museum in 1980

CONTENTS

INTRODUCTION

I made my first visit to the British Museum in 1921 when I came to London from Yorkshire with a scholarship to the Royal College of Art. The Museum was a revelation to me. I went at least twice a week for two or three hours each time, and one room after another caught my enthusiasm. The wonderful thing about the British Museum is that everything is stretched out before you and you are free to make your own discoveries.

By showing why particular pieces meant so much to me, I would like to think I could open other people's eyes to find inspiration for themselves. The pieces illustrated are a very restricted personal selection, but just as I would have been fascinated to know, say, what Picasso most liked in the Louvre and which works might have influenced him, so I hope people will be interested to see what has excited and influenced me in the British Museum. In my most formative years, nine-tenths of my understanding and learning about sculpture came from the British Museum.

In the twenties I wanted to get away from the emphasis on classical art which we had all around us in art school. In the British Museum I found what I was looking for in primitive, archaic and tribal art, and it is from these periods that I have chosen most work for reproduction. However, I have included some Greek sculpture because I did, and do, appreciate its greatness.

The pieces chosen have been picked out for a variety of reasons. People don't always realise that they should not be looking for, nor expect to find, the same qualities in every work of sculpture. Each individual work of art, in a way, emphasises some particular thing. A single work cannot and doesn't do everything. It would be ridiculous to expect that in a single work of art you could express vitality, peace, youth, violence, old age, etc. You can't get everything, but if you've got one thing intensified to the nth degree, then my goodness, you've got something. To compare a single individual carving of Michelangelo's, for example his Rondanini Pietà, with his painting of the Last Judgement (a narrative work containing hundreds of figures) is like comparing a single sonnet with a long novel like *War and Peace*.

Sculpture, painting and architecture

My personal choice in this book does not include relief sculpture, such as the wonderful Assyrian friezes or the Parthenon Frieze. As a young sculptor I looked upon relief sculptures as being more akin to painting and drawing, and I have always resented architects using relief sculpture just to embellish their buildings.

(*Left*) Henry Moore c.1923.

7

At art school we were always being told that architecture was the 'mother of the arts', implying that sculptors and painters were all dependent on jobs handed out from the architects. This I could never accept, for if there is a 'mother of the arts' it has been religion. Sculpture should never be considered a mere servant to architecture.

True full sculptural expression is through sculpture completely in the round, which has a great advantage over painting in that it can have back views, worm's-eye views, bird's-eye views; it can change with how the light falls on it, it can change with its surroundings, as it is seen by moonlight, sunlight or in rain. With a picture, on the other hand, the frame limits the area which you can connect with it. I realise that painting has many advantages over sculpture – besides the obvious one of the free use of colour with its great representational and emotional possibilities. It can represent distance, the sky, clouds, sunlight, darkness, water, and so on, unstable things which sculpture can't reproduce, but sculpture is more real to me – it is actual reality. I like making things that I know exist and that I have made as I intended. That is one reason why I make small maquettes before embarking on the final full-scale sculpture. With a small maquette a few inches in size you can turn it over in your hand and treat it almost as though you are a god creating something complete from every point of view.

Egyptian sculpture – its monumentality

Until I came to London the only real sculptures which I had seen (apart from plaster casts in art school) were the gothic heads on the porch of Methley Church, two miles from my birth town Castleford, so when I first visited the British Museum's Egyptian sculpture gallery, and saw the 'great arm' and imagined what the whole figure was like, which it had only been part of – then I realised how monumental, how enormous, how impressive a single piece of sculpture could be. Though it wasn't just the size alone which impressed me. Size and monumentality are not always the same thing. What I found in the Egyptian pieces was a monumentality of vision.

This is not something that can be taught; either artists have it or they don't. For example, Rubens has a monumental scale in all his work (all his women you would think were eight-footers) and we know with a Michelangelo figure, whatever size drawing he makes of it, that the figure in his mind's eye is over lifesize. Other artists, like Watteau for example, whose paintings I love – the women in his pictures you imagine to be at most 5 ft 6 in tall and they fit into ordinary life intimately, but not monumentally.

The Egyptians in their sculpture wanted to show that life has a greater significance than the ordinary daily routine of living. They managed to imbue a grandeur, a permanence, and some sort of religious meaning into their sculptures. I admire works of art which have this more-than-everyday feeling. When Cézanne paints two men playing cards, somehow they take on a nobility that raises everyday life to a height that gives a new faith in it, a new importance.

An early photograph of the Great Arm of Amenophis III in the old Egyptian Sculpture Gallery.

Moore's *King and Queen* of 1952–3, which was influenced by the seated Egyptian figures reproduced on pages 38–9.

Part of the grandeur of Egyptian sculpture comes also from the stillness, the timelessness of their poses. I like sculpture which does not represent actual physical movement, which is not jumping off its pedestal or starting a race. It seems to me that it's somehow against the nature of sculpture to be actually moving. I don't mind figures representing action in the Greek friezes or Assyrian relief sculptures of battle scenes, for, as I have said, these are more like pictures. But when it's a complete actual object, particularly in stone, representing movement seems false to me, and so I've never tried in my sculpture to make running or jumping figures. This doesn't mean there can be no life in a still figure. The Egyptian sculptures look as if they could move but are consciously sitting or standing still.

Sculpture in the twenties

To understand why the British Museum meant so much to me in the early 1920s it has to be remembered how little attention was given to sculpture in those days, either in the art colleges or among the general public.

If there is one special thing which perhaps pleases me about my career as a sculptor, it is that interest in my work may have helped towards the enormous growth in the appreciation and also the practice of sculpture in the last half century. When I began at Leeds School of Art they had to start a sculpture school specially for me and I was the only student. When I came to London to the Royal College of Art, there were only six or seven of us in the sculpture school, and for one year I had a large studio and a life model all to myself. Nowadays they have seventy applicants for each of the ten new places available every year for sculpture.

In the 1920s the only practising sculptor in England for whom I had any respect was Epstein, and I was fortunate that there were new ideas afoot about sculpture generally, which were to have a great impact on me. In 1920 Roger Fry had published his book *Vision and Design*, with its appreciation of primitive sculpture, and reading this book influenced me very much.

After I had finished my student course and was appointed to the teaching staff of the Royal College, I came to know Epstein quite well, and have never forgotten him taking me to his bedroom to see his collection of primitive carvings – it was so overflowing with negro sculptures etc. that I wondered how he got into bed without knocking something over.

In Paris, Picasso, Derain, Epstein, Brancusi and others had been collecting 'negro sculpture' for some years, but at the time I came to London it was only just becoming appreciated in England. (I would have liked to collect primitive sculpture myself, but though you could get a good African carving for £10 in the Caledonian market, my scholarship of only £90 a year put this beyond me.)

But although I myself could not afford to collect, there was a wealth of experience and inspiration to hand in the Ethnographical Galleries of the British Museum (now moved to the Museum of Mankind). The displays for me were wonderful; works were packed together in the glass show-cases, often jumbled up, and so on

(*Above*) Stone pestle from Papua New Guinea with (*right*) sketches from Henry Moore's Notebook No.3 (1922–4), showing how he developed sculptural ideas from his initial drawing.

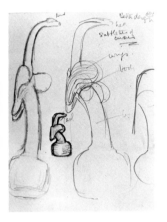

every visit there always seemed to be new things to discover. I was particularly interested in the African and Pacific sculptures and felt that 'primitive' was a misleading description of them, suggesting crudeness and incompetence. It was obvious to me that these artists were not trying – and failing – to represent the human form naturalistically, but that they had definite traditions of their own. The existence of such varied traditions outside European art was a great revelation and stimulus. I used to draw many of these carvings, sometimes on any scraps of paper I had with me, sometimes in sketchbooks. And, of course, some of these carvings influenced my own work later.

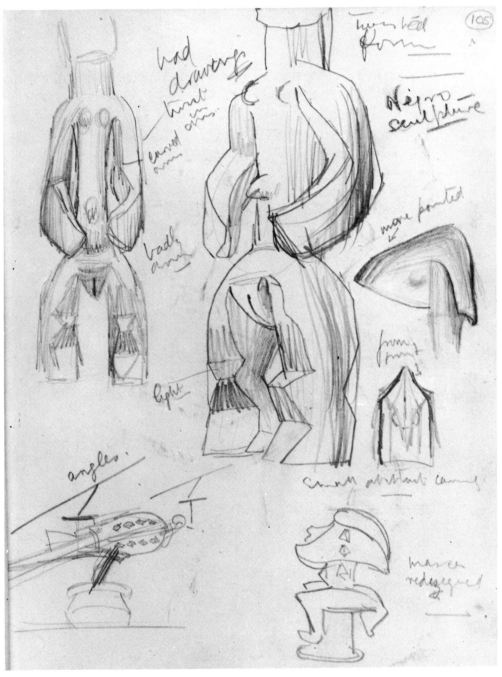

Page 105 from Henry Moore's Notebook No.3 (1922–4), showing his sketches of various items in the Museum's ethnographic collections.

Sense of touch

When I visited the British Museum recently to remind myself of favourite pieces, I was allowed to hold and touch many of the smaller ones – a wonderful experience. This, of course, is what museums can't generally allow people to do, but the sense of touch is very important in sculpture, a sense which we learn from the very beginning of our childhood. We learn from our mother's breast what is soft and round. We learn from our own knees what is hard, the bony things, and we learn what is prickly, or warm or cold. I think to hold a figure such as in the illustration here should be part of the experience of anyone who wants to appreciate and understand sculpture. They should hold it blindfolded, and then try to draw it without having seen it, so that their sense of touch and shape, from their hands alone, means something to them. (If human beings had never had hands, but something like horses' hooves instead, besides losing the ability to use tools, we could not have developed the sense of form that we have.)

Henry Moore with a Cycladic figure from the British Museum.

A sense of form – Cycladic sculpture and direct carving

If I was asked to explain to students what it is I mean by 'a sense of form' perhaps I would start off with the Cycladic Room of the British Museum, for what the Cycladic sculpture has got is an unbelievably pure sense of style, of unity of form. It's as though they couldn't go wrong, but always arrived at a result which was inevitable from the beginning. Another attraction for me of Cycladic sculpture was that most of it is in marble. Around 1910 to 1920 a strong belief came to be held by a few sculptors that they should carve directly in the material rather than casting their work into a different material, such as bronze.

For some centuries after the Renaissance, the practice had grown up for sculptors to employ the 'pointing machine' in producing work in marble or stone – that is, the sculptor first modelled in clay the work he intended to make, then this would be cast into plaster and the result was copied by the sculptor (or more often by a professional stone carver) by the use of a pointing machine (which

A letter from Henry Moore to Lord Eccles, then Chairman of the Trustees, in 1969, agreeing to exhibit one of his sculptures alongside Cycladic pieces in the Museum. The *Moon Head* he refers to is illustrated on page 47.

could take exact measurements from the plaster copy and transfer them to the marble copy). This general use of the pointing machine led to sculptors not understanding the natural qualities of marble or stone.

Henry Moore carving an early sculpture in his London studio, 1927.

This 'gospel' of 'direct carving' developed, through the work and ideas of sculptors like Brancusi (who had come to appreciate and be influenced by primitive art) and a few others. And I came to believe in 'direct carving' very strongly, even considering a stone sculpture was in itself better than a bronze or terracotta just because it was produced directly in stone. As a young sculptor, loving stone and enjoying the actual activity of carving, I was particularly impressed by the Mexican stone sculptures, for they seemed to me more 'stony' even than the Egyptian or Cycladic. Besides the physical pleasure I got in the use of a hammer and chisel, I also thought that since stone carving was a much slower process than working in clay, I had more time to consider what I was doing.

Nowadays I think it is not the material which the sculpture is made from, or even how it is made, which counts, but the vision or quality of mind and the

14

idea that's expressed through it. When young, and a beginner in carving, I also believed that stone should stay looking like a block of stone, until I went to Greece and handled some little marble Cycladic harp-players (dated around 2500 BC). Despite the hardness of the material and the lack of metal tools, the Cycladic sculptor had completely freed the arms and legs of the figure, and even the harp was freed from the original marble block. . . . I began to realise that there was no need for stone to restrict the expression of space as well as of form.

I began to move away from total devotion to stone carving when I discovered that stone was a limitation on developing ideas from forms which I saw in nature. In stone you can't do really thin legs on a standing figure without great danger of breakages, you can't make figures that are completely free standing, but there they are in nature. So later in life I took to working also in metal, so as not to restrict my experimenting with thin forms. I began to realise that it was wrong to work to any given theory, one must be free to develop.

I think that the greatest works are a mixture of art and nature. Every painter or sculptor learns, of course, from past art, and learns by emulating past art, but if he doesn't also look at nature, at the world around him, he may become just a pasticheur. If he only wishes to copy nature, it is easier to use a camera. But art has to go through the human mind.

Drawing and looking

I think drawing ought to be taught seriously, even in primary schools, as a general part of education, much more than it is, not with the idea of producing a lot of painters and sculptors, but to get people to look, to use their eyes. Children are taught that language is a way of communicating between minds, and that music is communication through the ears, but they are not taught to use their eyes to understand nature, and to get nourishment from the visual arts, sculpture and painting. If they are made to draw something, they have to look at it; they may make a very poor drawing, but what matters is that for a short time they have looked intensely at something.

I feel sorry for people who go through life never really seeing the world about them. Everyone thinks they look, but they don't; they don't have the time, or the training, to open their eyes to the marvellous world we live in. The whole value of all the arts is to develop our experiences of life through our senses; a sculpture, for example, can make us realise what wonderful forms and shapes there are in the world, and what can be invented by human beings.

People often fail to appreciate certain works of art because they think that art must be 'beautiful' and they have a preconceived idea of what beauty is. But beauty to me is having nature revealed, and nature has lots of sides, not all of them graceful, or whatever people think is beautiful. Nature has power, it has force, it has violence and pain – all these things. And even pain is necessary to understand what comfort means. Repose, similarly, can teach you about violence;

people must understand the opposite of something in order to know what it really is.

Some people also have difficulty in enjoying art which is not obviously representational. But out of the many thousands of years of man's known art in every quarter of the globe, the periods of naturalistic sculpture amount to only a tiny proportion. The later Greeks were consciously representational, but medieval artists weren't, nor were the Aztecs, nor the Africans. To get the most out of sculpture (or any art) you must begin with an open mind and be prepared to look again and again at a work before deciding whether or not you like it. You should look at it from many angles, you should concentrate for a while on some of the details; above all you must take time, and not hope to understand the true significance of a sculpture in a few seconds of casual looking.

Sometimes in my life I have hesitated in my work, even stopped doing things, because people liked them too easily. At one time I found that whenever I did a carving in alabaster, people said 'Isn't it beautiful?' – and I knew that they were only looking at the material, so I had to stop working in alabaster if I wanted people to look at the actual work for its sculptural form. There is a great deal still to be done with three-dimensional form as a means of expressing what people feel about themselves, and nature, and the world around them. But I don't think we shall, or should, ever get away from the basis that all sculpture is based on, i.e. the human body. For me personally, I need the human element – in that sense all my work is figurative.

In the preparation of this book, I toured the galleries with the photographer, David Finn, because I wanted to discuss with him the different pieces he was going to photograph. Photographing sculpture is a special art and I was delighted that a photographer so experienced in this field should have offered to help me. To make good photographs of paintings or drawings, one has, of course, to be a good photographer technically, to put it in a good even light and get the correct focus and exposure, but with sculpture one has to do more, one has to show its true form. The test of a good photograph of a sculpture is one from which another sculptor of equal merit could make a correct replica (given, of course, enough angles, for no single photograph can reveal the sculpture from all round). In this book, David Finn and I have sought to show not only the splendid form of the pieces themselves, but in some we also wanted to draw attention to special details.

It has been a wonderful experience for me to recapture the delight, the excitement, the inspiration I got in these pieces as a young and developing sculptor, and I envy my readers who still have these and their own discoveries to make.

PHOTOGRAPHING WITH HENRY MOORE

by David Finn

One of Henry Moore's favourite games is to ask friends in a social gathering to try to name the ten greatest artists of all time. Once on a long aeroplane ride together, I asked him to compose his own list. He discovered to his surprise that he could not restrict his list to ten. His greats numbered fifteen and he could leave none of them out in a final tally. His list consisted of Giotto, Giovanni Pisano, Massaccio, Van Eyck, Donatello, Piero della Francesca, Bellini, Leonardo, Raphael, Michelangelo, Dürer, Titian, Rembrandt, Rubens and Cézanne.

Over the years I have often talked to Henry Moore about his reaction to the works of his favourite (and not-so-favourite) artists, as well as different periods of art. He has told me of his first trip to Greece many years ago, which he still remembers so clearly (and is remembered with equal vividness by Professor Yalouris who showed him through Greek museums), and his special delight in seeing so many examples of Cycladic art. Moore recently told me of a trip to Mexico City and how amused and pleased he was when he was referred to as 'the greatest Mexican artist of our time'. He has described his visits as a young man to Brancusi's studio, his personal discovery of Rodin, his awe of Michelangelo. We have talked about Phidias and the fact that no one can say for sure what was done by his hand. He has told me of how as a young sculptor he thought little of Bernini and that not until much later in his life did he realise what a great sculptor Bernini was, how marvellously he handled stone, and how he, Henry Moore, had become bolder in his carving because of what he learned from studying Bernini's achievements.

Henry Moore's respect for 'the greatest artists' of the past has seemed to me to be a possible contradiction to his admiration for the unknown artists of ancient Greece, Africa, Mexico, New Guinea and other cultures, and I once asked him about this. He explained that his list could obviously only include known artists, and that there would be many more who would qualify if their names were recorded. Listening to him talk about the strength, the monumentality, the simplicity of form found in many works of unknown authorship, one can believe that he considers them as great as works by famous artists. The difference is only that we can know something about the personality of the latter as well as an extensive body of work that has an overall impact, whereas in the former, each work stands on its own.

I have rarely gone with Henry Moore to a museum to discuss at first hand his reaction to a work of art. He has told me about his impression of the 'Flying Horse' Chinese exhibition and 'Tutenkhamen', making the point that there are greater works in the permanent collection of the British Museum than in any of

the special exhibitions that create so much excitement. But in his home Moore talks eagerly about the works of art in his own collection. Once when I visited him, he became excited about the shadows thrown by the setting sun on an ancient sculpture of a lynx standing on his coffee table and asked me to quickly photograph the extraordinary forms of muscles and bones that were highlighted so wonderfully for a few brief moments. He has frequently referred to his Cézanne painting of 'Bathers', which he loves, and occasionally to his Courbet, Degas, Rodin and other works. He was as happy as any collector when he acquired a section of a thirteenth- or fourteenth-century pulpit, and more recently when he was able to acquire a cast of a large Oceanic sculpture from the British Museum (shown in this book on p.82) which he felt was so powerful that it was difficult to find the right place in his house to put it.

Over a period of twenty years, I have spent many hours with Henry Moore

Lynx owned by Henry Moore.

and watched him touch his sculpture, move his hands over favourite spots, look at work from different angles to satisfy himself that he has considered every view from which the sculpture might be seen. I have taken thousands of pictures of his sculpture, including almost every one of his major works and a great many of his smaller pieces. I have also photographed his sculpture in different environments in different parts of the world. And perhaps most importantly of all, I have reviewed with him hundreds of prints of those photographs in preparation for various books on his work. As a result I have come to know what he looks for in a picture, and to seek this myself as I look through the camera lens.

In a very real sense Henry Moore has been my teacher as well as my friend, a teacher who, in the best tradition of education, has taught me not to imitate but to develop my own powers of observation and discovery. My perceptions as a photographer have been sharpened by his sculptor's eye, and I find myself working in another medium, often with very different subject matter, but with an intuitive approach that is quite similar to his.

One way in which this shows itself is that I find those elements in nature which are most moving to me (and which I therefore pick out with my camera) are elements which attract his eye as well. Once I took a series of photographs of Stonehenge and, knowing of his lifelong love of those great stones, brought the pictures out to Much Hadham to show him. It so happened that when I arrived Stephen Spender was going over a new series of lithographs on Stonehenge which Moore had just completed and for which Spender was in the process of writing an introductory essay. I had not seen or even known about the lithographs before, and of course Moore had not seen my photographs. But as we looked over both collections it was quite startling to see how often we had picked out the same sections to depict.

The one difference in our point of view which is worth noting has to do with our attitude towards what makes a good photograph. As a sculptor, Moore sees photography as playing a specific role in his creative process. When he worked on the UNESCO commission, for instance, it was helpful, he once told me, to make an enlargement to the proposed size of a smaller sculpture which he thought had the right shape for the site. The photograph was a method of accomplishing a sculptural purpose. Over the years he has often made larger-than-lifesize prints of small maquettes as one way, perhaps, of deciding whether he wants to do a larger version of the work. He is quite studious in the way he sets up his own camera to take a photograph of a piece he has finished, and he enjoys seeing a print which describes the sculpture as he thinks it should be represented. So keen is he in the process of photographing that some years ago I bought for him a Hasselblad camera (which I use) with a collection of lenses, magazines, polaroid back, etc. I spent an afternoon teaching him how to use the camera, but in the end he found it too complicated and went back to his trusty Leica, turning the Hasselblad over to one of his assistants.

For Henry Moore a good photograph of sculpture is one which would enable him to do the sculpture over again if the original was lost. He sees it as a means rather than an end, whereas I naturally view photography as an artistic medium in its own right.

It is a great pleasure to me when through photographs I can discover secrets in different works of sculpture that Henry Moore and others will find revealing. That's why I was delighted at the opportunity to take the photographs for this book on the sculpture in the British Museum, which has meant so much to Moore since his days as an art student. I was sure that the sculpture he would identify would be equally moving to me and that photographing these works would be a uniquely rewarding creative experience. I was not mistaken.

Before embarking on the photography, we took a tour around the museum so that he could point out at first hand the objects he had selected. An observer might have expected to hear the sculptor tell the photographer to take this detail or that, to photograph from one or another angle, to consider a certain kind of lighting; but that was not necessary. I could readily see why the various objects were so compelling to Moore, and he knew that I would photograph the objects in a way that would be pleasing to him.

Subsequently I made many trips on my own for my photography project, in some instances photographing the objects as they were displayed, in others photographing them out of their cases and with special lighting. As I moved from room to room and period to period I was amazed to see the works Moore had selected. There is so much that is beautiful in the British Museum collection that anyone would have difficulty picking out his favourites, and I probably would have made a somewhat different choice. But in every instance I could see why Moore's selection made sense from his point of view. And often, as I was photographing an individual piece, I thought I could see where Moore may have gained an idea for one or another of his familiar sculptural passages from these particular works which he had spent so much time with as a young sculptor.

In the course of doing my work, I took far more pictures and made many more prints than I knew could possibly be used in the book, but I wanted Moore to make the selection rather than me. And so the final stage in preparing the material for the book was several sessions with him, going over all the photographs, commenting on the relative merits of different prints, and putting together a collection that expressed his point of view. I find the final selection to be an excellent one and hope that it will be helpful in pointing out to others what the finest qualities in these various works of art are – as Henry Moore and this particular photographer saw them. I know that working on this book meant a great deal to Moore because he has such a strong desire to help people learn to see and experience sculpture as he thinks they should. For me it was an extraordinarily rewarding experience to provide the camera eye through which his purpose could be served.

BIOGRAPHICAL NOTES

1898

Born Castleford, Yorkshire, 30 July, the seventh child of Raymond Spencer Moore, a coal miner, and of Mary Baker, his Staffordshire-born wife.

1902–10

Attended Castleford Primary school and won scholarship to the local Grammer school.

1915–16

Gained his Cambridge Senior Certificate and began studying to be a teacher.

Worked at his old school in Castleford.

1917

Joined the army (the Civil Service Rifles, the 15th London Regiment). Drafted to the Western Front in France.

Gassed at the Battle of Cambrai and returned to England. After some time in hospital he spent the rest of the war as a bayonet instructor.

Redrafted to France.

1919

After demoblisation returned to teaching.

Enrolled at Leeds School of Art where he studied for two years.

1921

Awarded scholarship to study sculpture at the Royal College of Art, London. Began to make frequent visits to the British Museum to study the sculpture collections.

1923

First of many visits to Paris, where he visited the Péllerin Collection.

1924

Granted Royal College of Art Travelling Scholarship.

Appointed instructor in the Sculpture School for a term of seven years.

1925

Six months travelling in France and Italy.

1926

First exhibition in a mixed show at the St George's Gallery, London.

1928

First one-man exhibition at the Warren Gallery, London.

Received first public commission, to carve a relief for the new Underground Building, at St James's London.

1929

Married Irina Radetsky, a student of painting at the Royal College of Art.

1930

Member of the 'Seven and Five Society'.

1931

One-man show at the Leicester Gallery, London.

First sale to the continent, to the Museum für Kunst und Gewerbe, Hamburg.

Bought cottage at Barfreston, Kent, for use during College vacations.

1932

Moved to the Chelsea School of Art to establish a department of sculpture.

1933

Became a member of the avant-garde group 'Unit One'.

1934

Left Barfreston to take a cottage with a large garden at Kingston near Canterbury where he could work in the open air.

Publication of the first monograph on his work (by Herbert Read).

1936

Took part in the International Surrealist Exhibition at the New Burlington Galleries.

Toured the cave paintings in the Pyrenees and Altamira, and visited Madrid, Toledo and Barcelona.

1938

Took part in the Exhibition of Abstract Art at the Stedelijk Museum, Amsterdam.

1939

Gave up teaching when the Chelsea School of Art was evacuated and lived full-time at Kingston.

1940

Returned to his London studio and began the famous series of *Shelter Drawings* inspired by the scenes in the underground stations as people sheltered from the Blitz.

Appointed Official War Artist.

When their London studio was bombed, the Moores bought a house near Much Hadham in Hertfordshire, where they have lived ever since.

1941

Appointed Trustee of the Tate Gallery.

Exhibition at Temple Newsam, Leeds.

1943

Commissioned to carve a *Madonna and Child* for St Matthew's Church, Northampton.

First one-man exhibition outside England at the Buchholz Gallery, New York.

1945

Appointed to the Art Panel of the British Council, London.

Made Honorary Doctor of Literature at Leeds University.

Visited Paris for the first time since the war.

Exhibition at the Berkeley Galleries, London.

1946

Birth of his only child, Mary.

Visited New York on the occasion of his first major retrospective exhibition, at the Museum of Modern Art.

1948

Awarded International Prize for Sculpture at the XXIVth Biennale, Venice.

Appointed member of Royal Fine Art Commission (1948 to 1971).

Elected Foreign Corresponding Member of the Académie Royale Flamande des Sciences, Lettres et Beaux-Arts de Belgique.

1950

Elected Foreign member of the Swedish Royal Academy of Fine Arts.

1951

First retrospective exhibition in London, at the Tate Gallery.

1953

Created Honorary Doctor of Literature, University of London.

Awarded International Prize for sculpture at the IInd Biennale, São Paulo and visited Brazil and Mexico.

1955

Appointed to the order of the Companions of Honour.

Appointed Trustee of the National Gallery, London (1955 to 1974).

Elected foreign honorary member of the American Academy of Arts and Sciences.

1957

Awarded prize at the Carnegie International, Pittsburg.

Awarded the Stefan Lochner Medal by the City of Cologne.

1958

Appointed Chairman of the Auschwitz Memorial Committee.

Created Honorary Doctor of Arts, University of Harvard.

1959

Created Honorary Doctor of Literature, University of Reading.

Created Honorary Doctor of Laws, University of Cambridge.

Awarded Gold Medal by the Society of the Friends of Art, Krakow.

Awarded Foreign Ministers prize at the Vth Biennale, Tokyo.

Nominated Corresponding Academician by the Academia Nacional de Bellas Artes, Buenos Aires.

1961

Created Honorary Doctor of Literature, University of Oxford.

Elected member of the American Academy of Art and Letters.

Elected member of the Akademie der Kunste, West Berlin.

1962

Elected Honorary Fellow of Lincoln College, Oxford.

Created Honorary Freeman of the Borough of Castleford.

Created Honorary Doctor of Engineering, Technische Hochschule, West Berlin.

Created Honorary Doctor of Letters, University of Hull.

1963

Appointed member of the Order of Merit.

Awarded the Antonio Feltrinelli Prize for sculpture by the Accademia Nazionale dei Lincei, Rome.

Elected Honorary Member of the Society of Finnish Artists.

1964

Awarded Fine Arts Medal by the Institute of Architects, U.S.A.

1965

Bought house at Forte dei Marmi, near Carrara.

Elected Honorary Fellow of Churchill College, Cambridge.

Created Honorary Doctor of Letters, University of Sussex.

1966

Elected Fellow of the British Academy.

Created Honorary Doctor of Laws, University of Sheffield.

Created Honorary Doctor of Literature, University of York.

Created Honorary Doctor of Arts, Yale University.

1967

Created Honorary Doctor of Laws, University of St Andrews.

Created Honorary Doctor, Royal College of Art, London.

Created Honorary Professor of Sculpture, Carrara Academy of Fine Art.

1968

Retrospective exhibition at Tate Gallery, London, on occasion of his 70th birthday.

Awarded the Erasmus Prize, The Netherlands.

Awarded the Einstein Prize by the Yeshiva University, New York.

Awarded the Order of Merit by the Federal German Republic.

Created Honorary Doctor of Laws, University of Toronto.

1969

Created Honorary Doctor of Laws, University of Manchester.

Created Honorary Doctor of Letters, University of Warwick.

Created Honorary member of the Weiner Secession, Vienna.

1970

Created Honorary Doctor of Literature, University of Durham.

1971

Created Honorary Doctor of Letters, University of Leicester.

Elected Honorary Fellow of the R.I.B.A.

1972

Retrospective Exhibition at Forte di Belvedere, Florence.

Created Honorary Doctor of Letters, York University, Toronto.

Awarded Medal of the Royal Canadian Academy of Arts.

Created Cavaliere di Gran Croce dell'Ordine al Merito della Repubblica Italiana.

Awarded the Premio Ibico Reggino Arti Figurative per la Scultura, Reggio Calabria.

1973

Awarded the Premio Umberto Biancamano, Milan.

Created Commandeur de l'Ordre des Arts et des Lettres, Paris.

1974

Opening of the Henry Moore Sculpture Centre at the Art Gallery of Ontario, Toronto.

Created Honorary Doctor of Humane Letters, Columbia University, New York.

Elected Honorary member of the Royal Scottish Academy of Painting, Sculpture and Architecture, Edinburgh.

1975

Created Honorary member of the Akademie der Bildenden Kunste, Vienna.

Elected Membre de l'Institut, Académie des Beaux Arts, Paris.

Awarded the Kaiserring der Stadt Goslar, West Germany.

Created Associate of the Académie Royale Flamande des Sciences, Lettres et Beaux-Arts de Belgique.

1977

Formed The Henry Moore Foundation.

Elected member of the Serbian Academy of Sciences and Arts.

1978

Major donation of sculptures to the Tate Gallery, London.

80th birthday exhibitions at the Serpentine Gallery and in Kensington Gardens, London and the City Art Gallery, Bradford.

Awarded the Grosse Goldene Ehrenzeichen by the City of Vienna.

Awarded the Austrian Medal for Science and Art.

1979

Created Honorary Doctor of Letters, University of Bradford.

1980

Donation of Large Arch to the Department of the Environment for permanent siting in Kensington Gardens.

Presented by Chancellor Schmidt with the Grand Cross of the Order of Merit of the Federal German Republic.

1981

Elected Full Member of Académie Européenne des Sciences, des Arts et des Lettres, Paris.

Major retrospective exhibition in Retiro Park, Palacio Velazquez and Palacio Cristal, Madrid; Gulbenkian Foundation, Lisbon; Miro Foundation, Barcelona.

Created Honorary Freeman of the City of Leeds.

THE PLATES

With commentary by Henry Moore

EGYPTIAN
SCULPTURE

Tetisheri, the grandmother of Amosis, first king of the Eighteenth Dynasty. Limestone statuette about 1575 BC.

'This is a little gem. I so admire the way the head-dress has been freed from the body so that you can look through its arches to the delicate neck inside. The sweetness of the face, the whiteness of the limestone and the simplicity of the pose all combine to give the impression of a fairy-tale princess.'

(*Overleaf*) Meryrehashtef, a provincial official of the Sixth Dynasty. Hard wood statuette, about 2200 BC.

'What I admire about this statue is its tension. If you run your hands down the legs or across the shoulder blades you can feel the tautness and hardness of the muscles. The Egyptian sculptor has squeezed tense physical energy into the whole piece.'

28

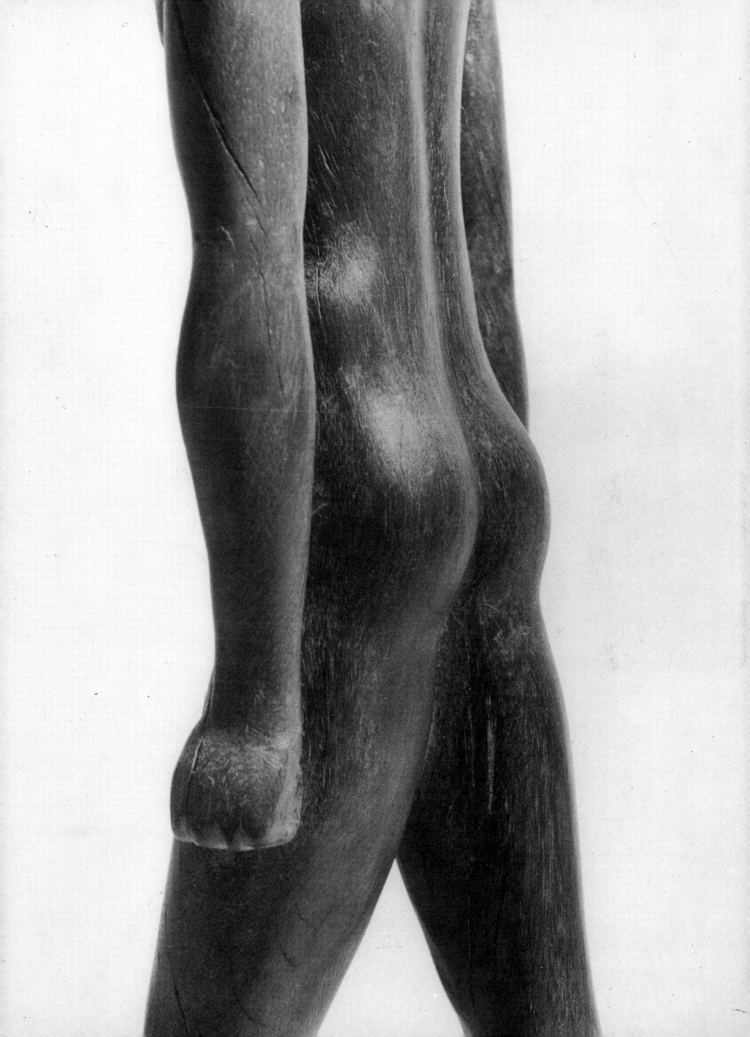

Grey granite figure of an official, late Twelfth Dynasty, about 1800 BC.

'Here the sculptor uses a cloak to show the body form, and by making one side fuller than the other he has given it a feeling of movement, as if the wearer had just pulled it closer around him. I also like the way the hand creeps out like a ghost from the material. A figure similar to this may well have influenced Rodin's cloaked statue of Balzac.'

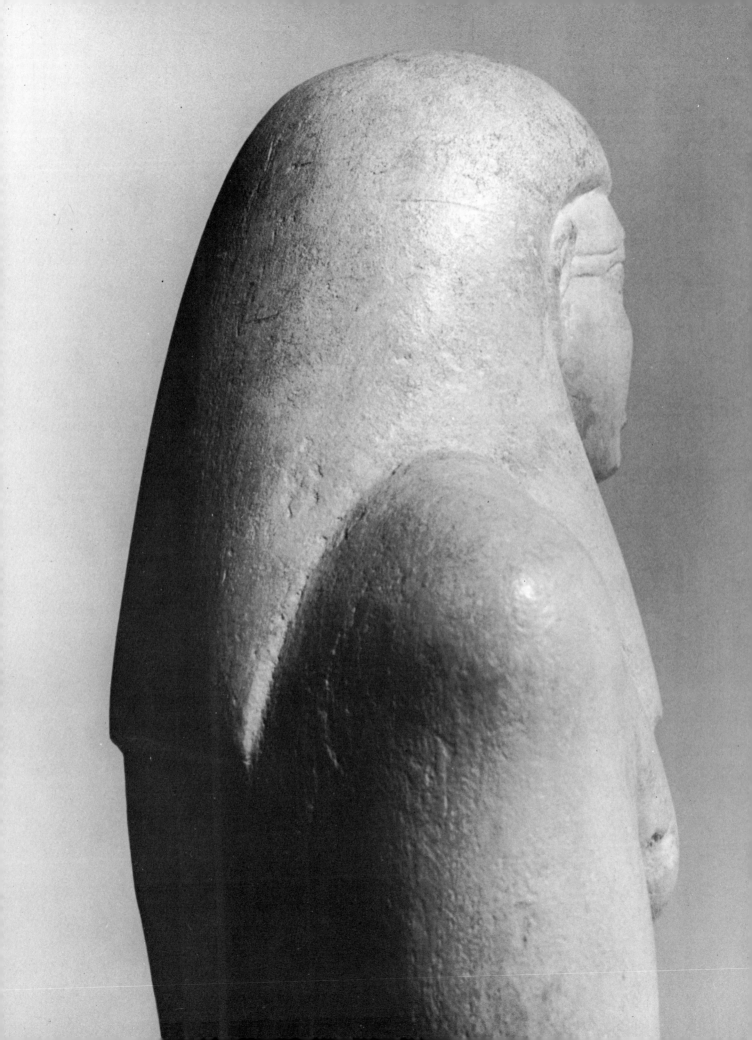

The chamberlain Inyotef, son of Senet.
Limestone figure of the Twelfth
Dynasty, about 1950 BC.

*'This piece shows tremendously fine
observation of the human figure, stylised
but realistic. The back [page 73] is equally
good – strong, taut and poised. The whole
figure has the stillness I particularly
associate with the Egyptians, a stillness of
waiting, not of death.'*

Painted, almost life-size figure of the high official Nenkheftka who lived during the Fifth Dynasty, about 2400 BC.

'This is another fine example of the tension in Egyptian sculpture. Look at the clenched fist and the braced legs. I like too the way the pleated kilt is used to emphasise the form of the body beneath.'

A high official and his wife, in hard white limestone. Late Eighteenth Dynasty, about 1340 BC.

'This has always been a great favourite of mine. For me these two people are terribly real and I feel the difference between male and female. The sculptor has done it in an obvious way by making the man slightly bigger than the woman, but it works, and this influenced me when I came to make my bronze King and Queen [see page 9]. It is such a pity the hands are damaged for, after the face, I think the hands are the most expressive part of the body. But even damaged the arms have a superb sense of repose and serenity which is so characteristic of Egyptian sculpture. Notice too that there are no marks of ageing on the faces. The pair are represented at an ideal age, one of full growth but before disillusionment has set in.'

(*Right*) Moore's *Animal Head*, 1956.

(*Below*) Alabaster head of a cow from Deir el-Bahari, about 1480 BC.

'*I chose this for its marvellous innocent simplicity. The sculptor has perfectly captured the soft docility of a young cow. The Egyptians had great feeling for animals and this is one I love.*'

(*Opposite*) Part of the head of a limestone statue, thought to represent King Akhenaten of the Eighteenth Dynasty (about 1355 BC).

'*This is a wonderful example of how a good sculptor can make his material look like a quite different substance. These lips look like soft, pliable, sensuous flesh, and yet they are carved in limestone. The realism is amazing, particularly in the tiny ridge along the edge of the lower lip.*'

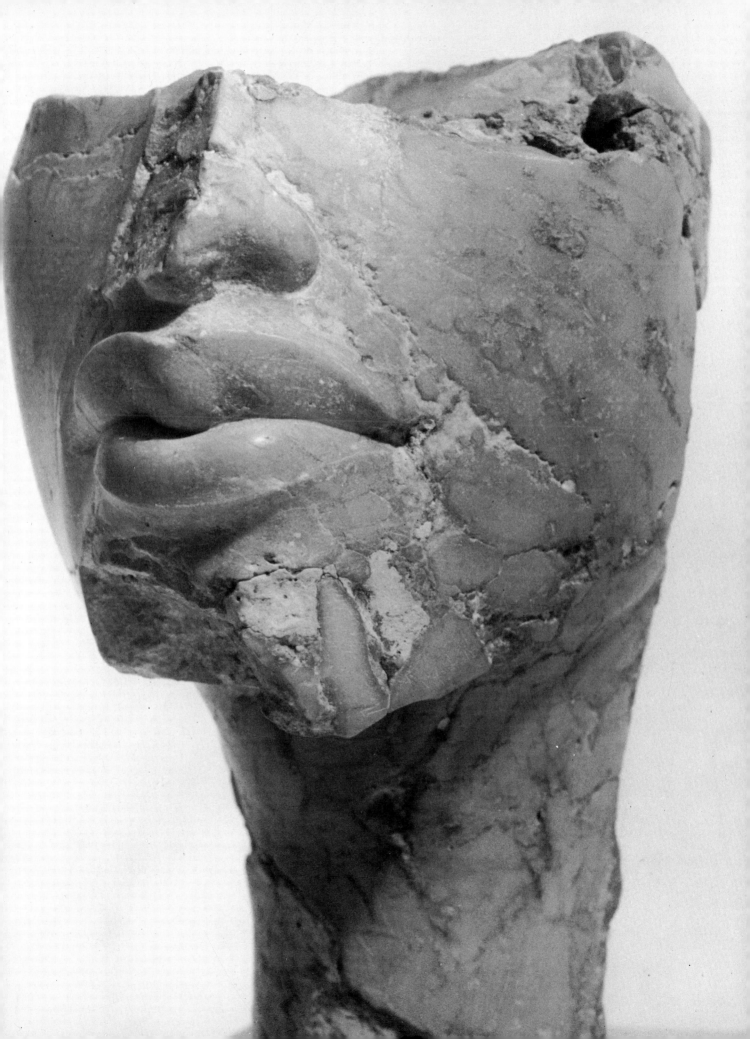

GREEK SCULPTURE

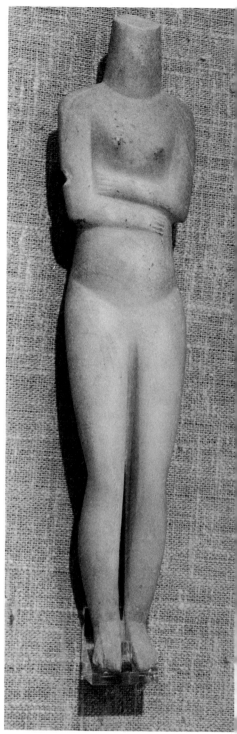

Cycladic marble figurines, about 2700–
2300 BC. The detail (*right*) is from the
left-hand figure. The small 'violin
idol' (*bottom right*) also represents a
woman.

*I simply love the innate sculptural sense of
these Cycladic figures. It's as though the
sculptor can't make a mistake, never
arrives at a result that was not inevitable
at the beginning. See how the little violin
figure expresses the kernel of the style
which is developed and refined in the larger
figures. Although the images appear to be
standing still, there is just a little
suggestion of movement, particularly in
the headless woman [left], whose knees are
coming forward.*

   *Despite the simplicity of the form, the
figures are very female in feeling; look at
the lovely long legs of the headless lady
and the full thighs of both figures. In order
to create the pose with folded arms, one
arm has to be shorter than the other from
shoulder to elbow, but each piece is so
beautifully unified in technique and vision
that the eye accepts it easily.'*

45

Left) Cycladic jug, about 1850–1700 BC.

Right) Cycladic marble collared jar, about 3200–2700 BC.

Below right) Moore's sculpture *Moon Head*, 1964, which was at one period exhibited in the Museum beside examples of Cycladic sculpture which had influenced it (see the letter illustrated on page 13).

'The shape of these vases shows the great inventiveness of the Cycladic sculptors. In the marble jar on the right, for example, the stand echoes the shape of the top. The one on the left shows how sculptural pottery can be. This piece is strongly figurative with a body, neck and head, and two little breasts at the front. There is no doubt our sense of form comes from our own bodies. If we didn't have a head and body, two arms and two legs, feet and hands, the whole basis of plastic art would be quite different.'

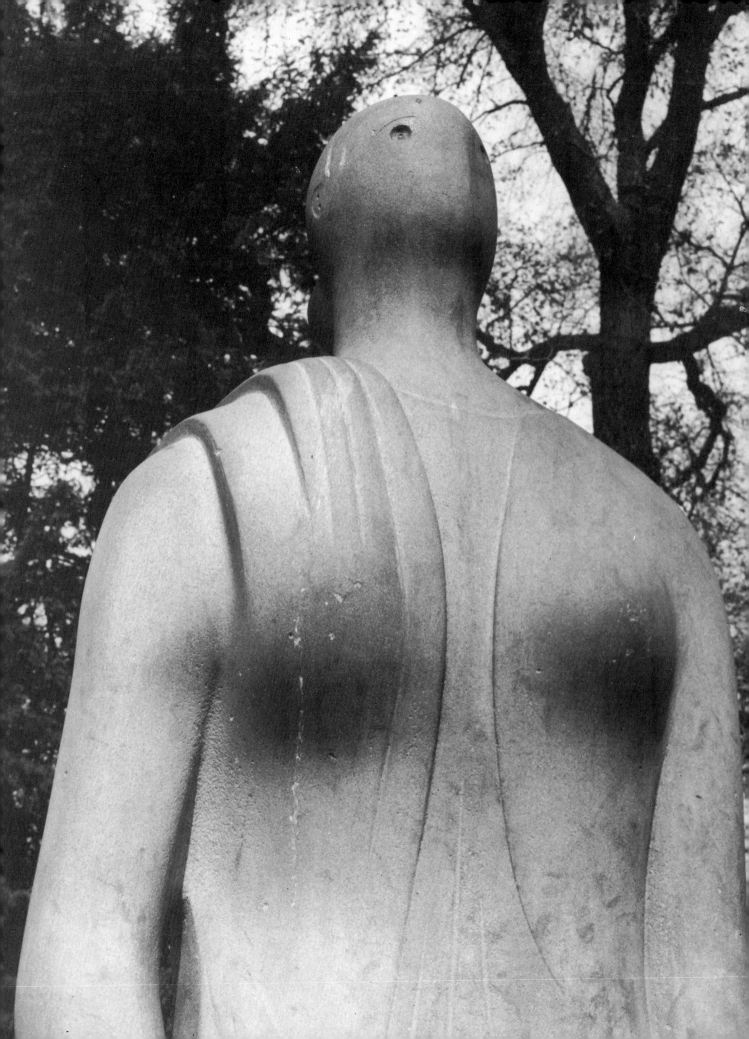

Four seated marble figures, made between 580–510 BC.

(*Previous pages*) Detail of headed figure, and one of Henry Moore's *Three Standing Figures*, 1947–8.

'When I was a student I often came and sat opposite one of these large figures. They weren't grouped together like this in the 1920s but I think this new arrangement of them is marvellous, it really emphasises their sense of repose and monumentality. Look how poised yet relaxed that simple head is, it's the very essence of a head on a neck on shoulders. I was always attracted to seated figures because, being immobile, they seemed essentially right for stone carving, which I thought should not try to represent actual movement. To make a running figure out of stone seemed to me to be a contradiction of reality.'

Bronze statuette of a horse with an armed rider.
Greek workmanship, made in Southern Italy about
550 BC.

(*Right*) Moore's *Nuclear Energy*, 1964, shows his
interest in helmet forms (see also his comments on
the Egyptian statuette, pages 28–9).

*'I love the vitality and alertness of this piece. You feel
that the horse could turn its head at any moment. I also
like the way the tail comes back towards the foot, to keep
the unity of the piece. Notice that because this is bronze
the legs can be thin and prancing; this you just could not
do in stone.'*

Marble lion that originally crowned a
tomb near Cnidus (south–west Asia
Minor). 3rd–2nd century BC.

*'This colossal sculpture really conveys the
serene majesty of the king of the jungle.
The face is marvellous, that nose is almost
breathing.'*

Gypsum statue of a woman from Vulci in Etruria. Etruscan, 570–560 BC.

'The face of this woman, and the stiffness of her pose, expresses for me a feeling of stark despair, like Lot's wife turned into a pillar of salt. She might be the heroine of a Greek tragedy. The rest of the figure is simply a column to support the head and the arms.'

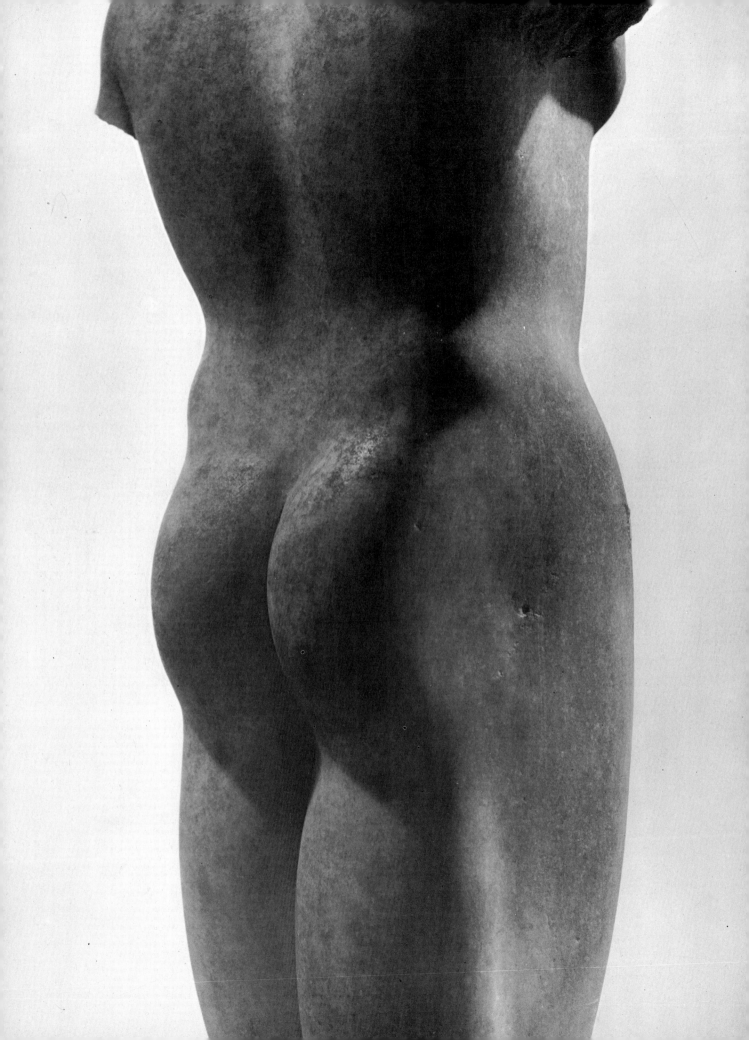

Marble torso of a youth. Greek, about
20 BC.

*This is a favourite Greek torso of mine,
and nowadays is so beautifully lit in the
Museum's display that its tense,
concentrated energy can be really
appreciated. Look how taut it is, how this
young boy is drawing in his stomach, and,
from the back, see how the buttocks are
nipped in like nutcrackers. It is motionless
and yet it oozes energy.'*

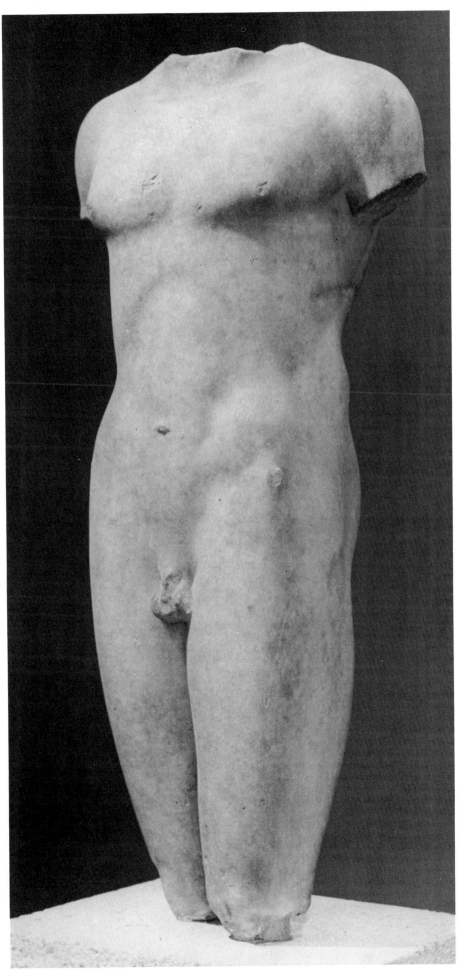

Reclining figure from the East
Pediment of the Parthenon at Athens,
438–432 BC. The figure probably
represents Herakles reclining on a
lion's skin but could be Dionysus.

*'The sculptor who did this had a thorough
understanding of the human figure, and
shows so realistically the difference between
the slackness of flesh and the hardness of
the bone beneath it. I knew, as a young
sculptor, that I had to learn all I could
about the human figure, but I rather took
the Greeks for granted and didn't realise
till much later how deep was their
observation of human form. But this piece
always attracted me, perhaps because of my
interest in reclining figures.'*

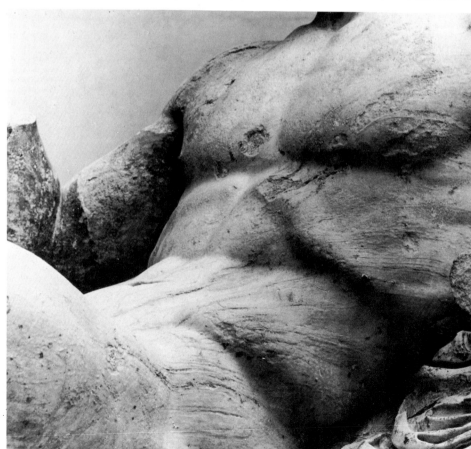

Marble 'Nereid', originally placed between columns of the Nereid Monument. From Xanthos in Lycia, about 400 BC.

(*Right*) Moore's *Draped Torso*, 1953.

'The drapery here is so sensitively carved that it gives the impression of light, flimsy material, wet with spray, being blown against the body by the wind. It shows how drapery can reveal the form more effectively than if the figure were nude because it can emphasise the prominent parts of the body, and falls slackly in the hollows. This is something I learned when I came to do the Shelter drawings, in which all the figures are draped. Before then I avoided using drapery because I wanted to be absolutely explicit about shapes and forms. I so admire the Greek sculptor who had the vision and the ability to make of stone something so apparently flimsy as the drapery on this figure.'

AZTEC SCULPTURE

'The simple, monumental grandeur of Aztec carvings has appealed to me enormously
ever since I was a young student. It has a massive weightiness which you feel is
indestructible, and which is so true to the nature of stone. For this reason I felt, in the
1920s, that the Mexican pieces were the stoniest examples of stone sculpture ever made.
It was almost a fetish with me that the making of a sculpture should be conditioned by the
material used, that you shouldn't try to make stone represent an idea that could be more
naturally done in wood or in clay. This was one reason why the reclining figure appealed
to me, it was so suitable for stone carving. Nowadays I feel it is the artist's vision that
matters more than the material used, and I have chosen some pieces in this book which
use stone in an astonishingly unstony way (see pages 41 and 62).'

Aztec stone carvings from Mexico, 14th or 15th centuries.

(*Above and opposite*) Vessel (chacmool) in form of reclining man.

(*Overleaf left*) A seated man; (*right*) the god of death.

(*Left*) Henry Moore's *Memorial Figure*, 1945–6.

(*Left*) Back view of Aztec figure on
pages 71 and 68.

(*Right*) Back view of Moore's *Draped
Seated Woman*, 1957–8.

(*Right*) Back view of Egyptian figure
on page 34.

'Often people forget to look at the back of a
sculpture, and sometimes pieces are so
displayed that this is impossible. But a
back can be very expressive. Look how
relaxed the Aztec back is compared with
the upright posture of the Egyptian figure.'

(*Right and above*) Rattlesnake.

'*Although the snake is coiled into a most solid form, it has a real air of menace, as if it could strike at any moment.*'

(*Opposite*) Stone mask of Xipe Totec.

'*This is a very unusual, marvellous piece. The sculptor has used the hole (as I personally did when I came to make holes) to make a formal contrast to the solid part of the sculpture; the space held inside should be appreciated as a shape in itself.*

74

OCEANIC
SCULPTURE

Easter Island stone statue of 'Hoa-Haka-Nana-Ia' ('Breaking Waves'), collected during the visit of HMS *Topaze* in 1868.

'*What a tremendous presence this figure has got. On Easter Island it was raised on a platform, and one can imagine the impression of power, dignity and authority it conveyed to the people below. I remember it when it stood on the colonnade of the British Museum but now it has an equally impressive position in the main hall of the Museum of Mankind. The Hawaiian sculptors knew instinctively that a sculpture designed for the open air had to be big. I always make my pieces larger than life-size if they are to be displayed out-of-doors because otherwise the immensity of sky, or a carpet of grass, dwarfs them into insignificance. Raising a sculpture can also help its impact, of course. It will appear far more monumental set against the sky than placed in a hollow on the ground.*'

painted wooden carving
commemorating the dead.
from New Ireland, Papua
New Guinea.

(*Right*) Henry Moore's carving
Internal-External Forms,
1952-3.

'*New Ireland carvings like this
made a tremendous impression on
me through their use of forms
within a form. I realised what a
sense of mystery could be achieved
by having the inside partly hidden
so that you have to move round
the sculpture to understand it. I
was also staggered by the
craftsmanship needed to make
these interior carvings. The so-
called primitive peoples were often
just as advanced in technique as
the more developed societies.*

*The painting of these pieces is
very attractive but, for me,
decoration on sculpture can be a
distraction from the impact of the
three-dimensional form. Many of
the sculptures in this book were
once painted but I often prefer
them in the natural stone or wood
as they appear today.*'

Wooden god from the Austral Islands, probably representing A'a, the principal deity of Rurutu. Inside the detachable back is a cavity where smaller images were originally kept.

This piece has such a fascination for me that I have had a bronze cast made of it which stands in the hall of my home. The little images, scattered all over the body like frogs jumping from a pool, are not stuck on but are all part of the same piece of wood – a remarkable technical achievement. And each figure is a separate piece of invention [see overleaf]. *The excitement of this piece comes from its sense of life-force, with all those small figures springing from the parent figure. The head, too, is marvellous. Its great round back repeats the shape of the full, round belly, but emphasises, by contrast, the thinness and sharpness of the jaw. On my cast I have made up the edge of the chin, where it is damaged in the original, because I so like its razor sharpness.'*

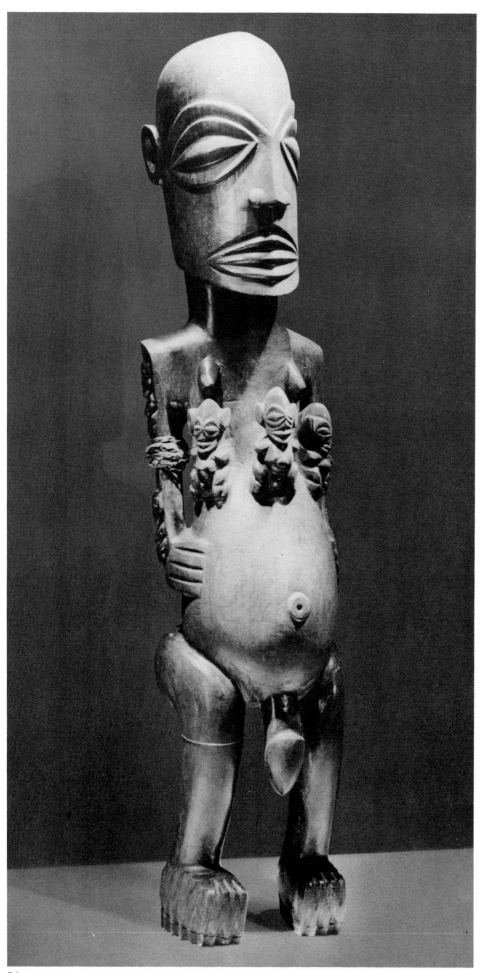

Wood figure of a god, perhaps Tangaroa, the sea-god and creator. From Rarotonga, Cook Islands.

'What a marvellous sense of style the Pacific sculptors had. Look at the unity of the eyes and mouth, the sharp edges of the nose and of the chin (similar to the previous figure). And I like the way the little figures are grouped on the chest, as if he were showing off his medals.'

(*Overleaf*) Hawaiian wooden image of a deity, with Henry Moore's drawing of it on page 90 of his No.3 Notebook, 1922–4.

'This has been a favourite of mine ever since my student days. It used to be exhibited in a large case with thirty or more other pieces but even then its amazing strength of form stood out and I felt I had to sketch it. It has the flat back and powerful muscles of a gorilla, combined with the tension and strain of a wrestler. It really is a marvellous piece.'

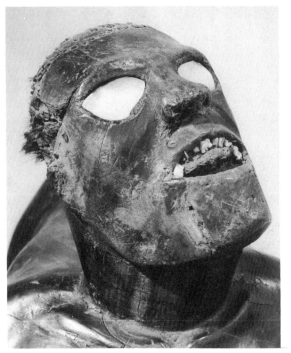

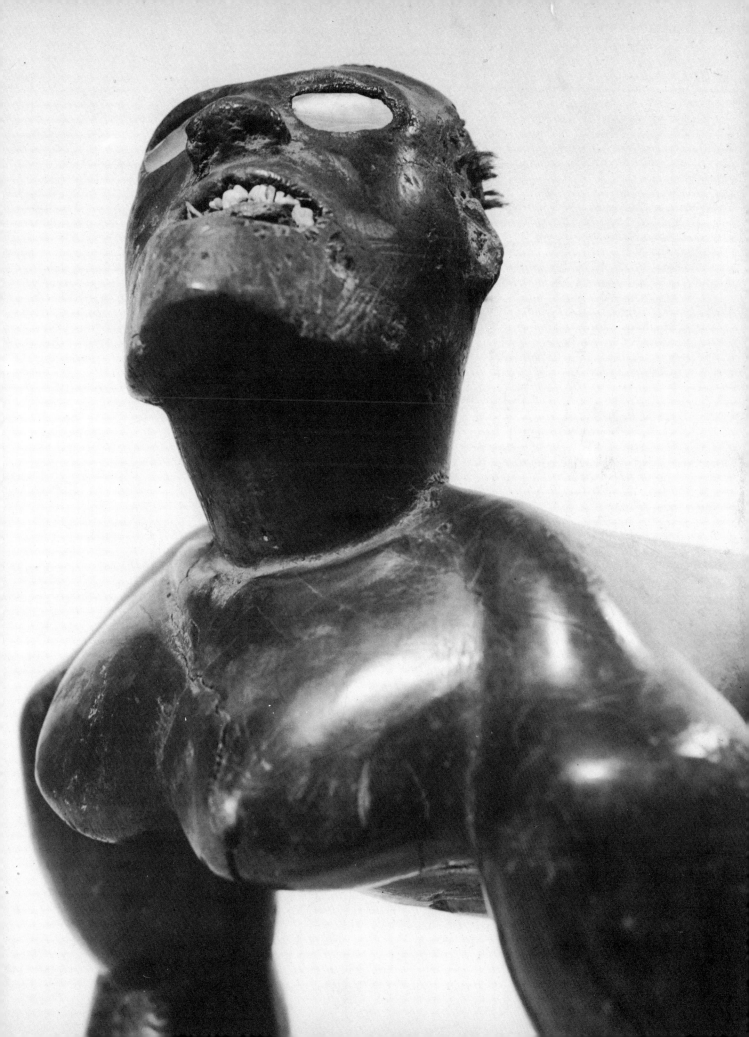

(*Left*) Wood figure from the Karawari River, Papua New Guinea.

(*Right*) Wood carving representing a war and hunting spirit, from the same area.

These two pieces show the remarkable individuality of the New Guinean sculptors. They have a sort of weirdness which I very much associate with the art of that part of the world. Whereas African sculpture is bulky, powerful, and solid, seeming to reflect a down-to-earth attitude to life, the Oceanic peoples appear to me to have a more anxious, nervous, over-imaginative view of the world, expressing itself in fantastic, birdlike, beetlelike forms with a nightmarish quality about them.'

AFRICAN SCULPTURE

(*Previous pages*) Male and female wood figures from Azande, southern Sudan.

'*What a remarkably inventive interpretation of arms, shoulders, elbows and fingers appears in these two pieces. To discover, as a young student, that the African carvers could interpret the human figure to this degree but still keep and intensify the expression, encouraged me to be more adventurous and experimental. There is nothing casual about the convention used; the sculptor enjoyed making the arms look like this, it was a deliberate achievement like writing a poem.*'

Double-headed dog and human figure from Bakongo, Zaire. These carvings were regarded as repositories of good or evil influences which might be manipulated by driving nails and blades into the body of the object.

'*These pieces are a complete reversal of the New Ireland carvings on pages 80–81. Instead of working inwards from the basic sculpture, these work outwards, as more and more nails are added to the body. It is fascinating that, though the additions were not in the sculptor's control, they have enhanced the existing form, not destroyed it.*'

(Previous pages) Wood figure from Baluba, Zaire, representing a female ancestor.

'*This is a very complete little figure; the sculptor had a clear idea of what he wanted to do. There must have been a long tradition of such sculptures in Baluba for this one to be as perfect and complete as it is. The long body, the short legs, are not signs of the sculptor's incompetence but of a tradition which exaggerated some parts of the body and underplayed others. The head is lovely, particularly the way the shape of the eyes repeats the shape of the head, and the division of the neck into repeating rings.*'

Wooden stool in the form of a kneeling woman, from Zaire, with Moore's sketch made in 1922-4.

(Overleaf) (left) Detail of above; *(right)* head-rest from the same area.

'*This is wonderful, a complete unified vision. Its proportions are quite unlike the human figure, yet it has more vitality and expression than a realistic figure would have. Look especially at the marvellous face, what an impression of stoicism and endurance it gives. The head-rest shown overleaf is a most complex, ingenious composition, with the same unity of style.*'

101

Chibinda Ilunga, the mythical hero-figure of the Bajokwe people, Angola.

'The remarkable invention of this piece extends even to the back of the head. It is typical of the solid, but expressive, three-dimensional approach of African sculptors, which I have always particularly admired. The Africans never worked in outline, they looked always into the middle of their subject, taking out the parts they wanted to depress and leaving the parts they wanted to project. After watching African carvers at the 1924 Wembley exhibition I decided it was their use of an adze, rather than an axe, that enabled them to work in this way, and I designed one to use myself. But my design lacked experience of how an adze works and quite soon it slid off the wood and onto my leg – I have the mark still. That adze was never used again!'

Wood helmet mask, said to represent a female spirit. From Baga, Guinee.

This piece has a splendidly self-satisfied air, as if she knows she's looking good. The head is very fine. See how the ear repeats the length from front to back of the head, rather than the width from side to side, and how in shape it repeats the back of the head, while the nose repeats the shape of the front. Here is a wonderful unity of form.'

Benin head of a Queen Mother, Nigeria. Heads of this form are usually dated to the 16th century AD. They were cast by the lost-wax process for use at the court of the Oba or ruler of Benin. The head shows the bead head-dress and collar worn by the ruler and queen mothers.

I love the womanly dignity of this piece and the beautiful details of its finish. The face is lovely but it was the views of the side and back as well, the perfection of its three dimensions, which first fascinated me. It has a sophisticated elegance which is most unusual in African sculpture.'

AMERICAN AND CARIBBEAN SCULPTURE

(*Left and right*) Arawak standing figure, from Jamaica.

(*Overleaf*) Arawak seat in the form of a male figure, from the Dominican Republic, with a page from Henry Moore's No.3 Notebook, 1922-4, showing his sketch of the seat alongside a drawing of the Hawaiian figure (page 88).

'*I well remember these Caribbean pieces from my student days. They were high up on a shelf so one could not see them fully, but I was able to draw the stool shown overleaf. I liked this partly because it was a reclining figure and partly for the freedom of the legs, they have so much life in them. The large figure shown on this page is tremendously expressive, even to the extent that tears have carved rivers down the face.*'

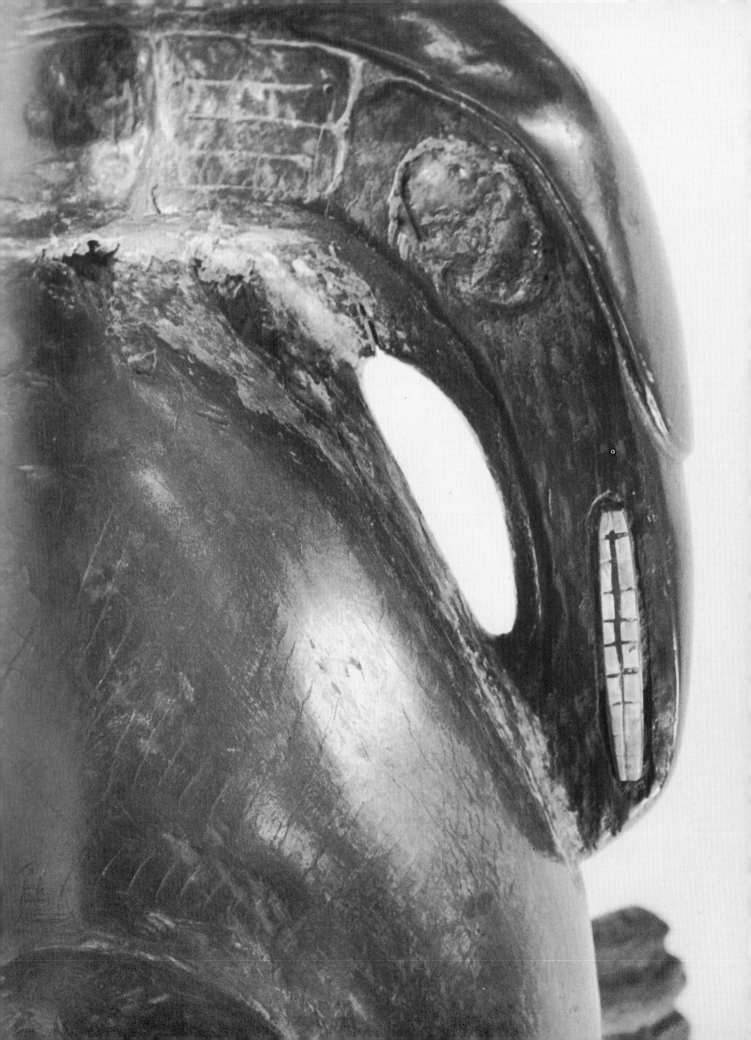

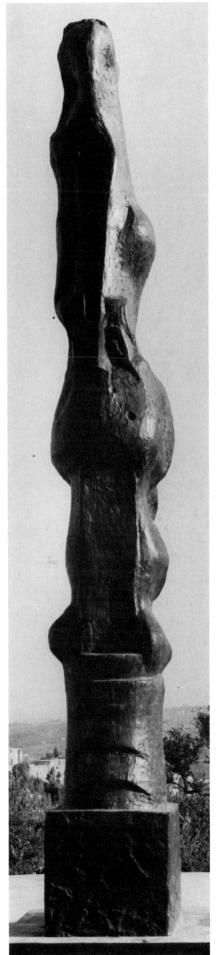

(*Left and above*) Arawak bird man, from Jamaica.

'*What I liked about this was the way the sculpture was built up in divisions, lump upon lump, as though it were breathing in matter, up from the toes, along the arms from the fingers, into the great swelling chest.*'

(*Right*) Henry Moore's *Upright Motive*, 1955–6.

Nootkan alderwood bowl, from
British Columbia.

*'This is a fine example of how you can
open up a single piece of wood in a way
which would be impossible with stone.'*

(*Left, right and overleaf*) Nootkan figures of mother and child, from Vancouver Island, British Columbia.

'The mother-and-child theme in sculpture is a universal one (and happens to be one of my repeated themes). It poses for the sculptor the relationship of a large form to a small one, and the dependency of the small form on the larger. Its appeal lies particularly in its expression of two basic human experiences: to be a child and to be a parent. These North American mother-and-child figures are remarkable. There is a great feeling of maternal protectiveness but they are not at all sentimental. Look how one child has a finger in its mother's eye!'

(*Left*) Henry Moore's *Family Group*, 1948–9.

(*Right*) Nootkan mother and child.

(*Below*) Detail from page 103 of the No.3 Notebook, 1922–4 showing a sketch of the Nootkan figure illustrated on pages 120–1.

LIST OF ILLUSTRATIONS

All photographs are by David Finn unless otherwise stated.

Frontispiece Henry Moore in front of the British Museum, 1980.

Page 6 Henry Moore c.1923. (Photo by courtesy of Ann Garrould)

Page 9 (*Above*) Fist of the left arm of a colossal royal statue in red granite, brought with the head of the statue from Karnak in Egypt, where the dismembered torso still lies. The royal owner has been variously identified as Tuthmosis III, Amenophis II, and Amenophis III of the Eighteenth Dynasty, and Ramesses II of the Nineteenth Dynasty, with dates extending from about 1480 BC to 1220 BC. Width of fist 46 cm. No.949. (Photo by courtesy of the Trustees of the British Museum) (*Below*) Henry Moore's *King and Queen*, 1952-3, bronze. Glenkiln, Shawhead, Dumfriesshire, Scotland.

Page 10 Stone pestle from Papua New Guinea. (Photo by courtesy of the Trustees of the British Museum)

Page 11 Pages 105-7 and 113 from Henry Moore's Notebook No.3, 1922-4. (Photo by courtesy of the Henry Moore Foundation)

Page 12 Henry Moore with a Cycladic figure from the British Museum.

Page 13 Letter from Henry Moore to Lord Eccles, 1969. (Photo by courtesy of the Trustees of the British Museum)

Page 14 Henry Moore in his London studio, 1927. (Photo by courtesy of the Henry Moore Foundation)

Page 18 Lynx owned by Henry Moore.

Egyptian Sculpture

Pages 26-7 see pp.38-9

Pages 28-9 Tetisheri, the subject of this limestone statuette, was grandmother of Amosis, the founder and first king of the Eighteenth Dynasty. It was made probably in the late Seventeenth Dynasty (c.1575 BC) and dedicated to Tetisheri by a member of her household. There are, however, many strange features about the piece which make a close dating difficult to achieve. Height 35.5 cm. No.22558.

Pages 30-1 Hard wood statuette of Meryrehashtef, a provincial official of the Sixth Dynasty (c.2200 BC). It is one of three figures found in Meryrehashtef's tomb at Sedment in Middle Egypt by Sir Flinders Petrie. It was presented to the Museum by the National Art-Collections Fund in 1923. Height 51 cm. No.55722.

Pages 32-3 Figure in grey granite of an official wearing a long cloak closely enveloping his body. There is no identifying inscription on the figure, but the base, now missing, may have carried a text. It is said to have come from Benha in the Egyptian Delta, and may be dated to the late Twelfth Dynasty (c.1800 BC). Height 62 cm. No.1237.

Pages 34-5 Limestone seated figure of the chamberlain Inyotef, son of Senet. It comes, with three funerary stelae also in the British Museum, from the mortuary chapel or cenotaph set up at Abydos by Inyotef. He exercised his office during the reign of Sesostris I of the Twelfth Dynasty (c.1950 BC). Height 65 cm. No.461.

Pages 36-7 Almost life-size limestone figure of the high official Nenkheftka who lived during the Fifth Dynasty (c.2400 BC). The wig is painted black, the exposed flesh a brownish red, and the kilt white. It was excavated from the tomb of Nenkheftka at Deshasha in Middle Egypt by the Egypt Exploration Fund, and presented to the Museum in 1897. Height 1.30 m. No.1239.

Pages 38-9 Seated pair-statue in hard white limestone of a high official and his wife. The absence of inscriptions and the incomplete carving of detail on the wigs and elsewhere, suggest that the piece is unfinished, possibly because the owner fell from grace, or even achieved notably higher status. It probably comes from Saqqara, and may be dated to the late Eighteenth Dynasty (c.1340 BC). Height 1.30 m. No.36.

Page 40 (*Above*) Henry Moore's *Animal Head*, 1956, bronze. Kröller-Müller Museum, Otterlo, The Netherlands. (*Below*) Egyptian alabaster head of a cow from the mortuary temple of Queen Hatshepsut at Deir el-Bahari (c.1480 BC). The eyes and eyebrows were inlaid with glass and coloured stones, and the horns were added probably in gilded wood or metal. A shrine to the goddess Hathor in cow-form was included in this temple. Excavated by the Egypt Exploration Fund, and presented to the Museum in 1905. Height 38.5 cm. No.42179.

Page 41 Lower part of the head of a statue of indurated limestone, generally considered to represent the King Akhenaten of the Eighteenth Dynasty (c.1355 BC). It was found in the ruins of the Temple of the Aten at El-Amarna in the mid-nineteenth century, and presented to the Museum by J. S. Perring in 1853. Height of surviving part 16 cm. No.13366.

Greek Sculpture

Pages 42-3 see pp.52-3

Page 44 (*Right*) Marble statuette of a woman, Cycladic, c.2700-2300 BC. Height 40 cm. GR 1875.3-13.1, Catalogue of Sculpture A 25.

Pages 44-5 Marble statuette of a woman, Cycladic, c.2700-2500 BC. Height 76.8 cm. GR 1971.5-21.1.

Page 45 (*Below*) 'Violin idol', stylised marble figurine representing a woman, from Amorgos. Cycladic, *c*.2700-2500 BC. Height 11·1 cm. GR 1889.5-21.2, Catalogue of Sculpture A 7.

Page 46 Cycladic jug with narrow neck and tilted spout, *c*.1850-1700 BC. Height 40·2 cm. GR 1920.10-15.1, Catalogue of Vases A 342.

Page 47 (*Above*) Marble collared jar, Cycladic, *c*.3200-2700 BC. Height 26·1 cm. GR 1843.5-7.76. (*Below*) Henry Moore's *Moon Head*, 1964, bronze. Private collection. (Photo by courtesy of the Henry Moore Foundation)

Page 48 Detail of one of Henry Moore's *Three Standing Figures*, 1947-8, Dale stone. Battersea Park, London.

Pages 49-51 Four seated marble figures that originally lined the Sacred Way from Miletus where it approached the Temple of Apollo at Didyma. Greek, *c*.580-510 BC. GR 1859.12-26.10, Sculpture B 271; GR 1859.12-26.5, Sculpture B 278; GR 1859.12-26.3, Sculpture B 276; GR 1859.12-26.9, Sculpture B 280.

Page 52 (*Below*) Henry Moore's *Nuclear Energy*, 1946, bronze. University of Chicago, Illinois, U.S.A.

Pages 52-3 Bronze statuette of a horse with an armed rider (*or a cavalryman*). Found at Grumentum in Lucania and probably made in Southern Italy *c*.550 BC. Greek workmanship. Height 25·4 cm. GR 1904.7-3.1.

Pages 54-5 Colossal marble lion that originally crowned a monumental tomb near Cnidus (south-west Asia Minor) 3rd-2nd century BC. Height 18·3 m. GR 1859.12-26.24, Catalogue of Sculpture 1350.

Pages 56-7 Gypsum statue of a woman found in a rich tomb in the Polledrara necropolis at Vulci in Etruria. Etruscan, 570-560 BC. Height 92·8 cm. GR 1850.2-27.1, Catalogue of Sculpture D 1.

Pages 58-9 Marble torso of a youth (kouros), Greek, *c*.520 BC. Found near the entrance to a tomb at Marion in Cyprus. Height 72 cm. GR 1887.8-1.1, Sculpture B 325.

Pages 60-1 Reclining marble figure from the East Pediment of the Parthenon, 438-432 BC. Height 1·25 m. GR 1816.6-10.93.

Page 62 (*Below*) Henry Moore's *Draped Torso*, 1953, bronze. Ferens Art Gallery, Hull. (Photo by courtesy of the Henry Moore Foundation)

Pages 62-3 Marble figure of a Nereid from the Nereid Monument, *c*.400 BC. Height 1·4 m. GR 1848.10-20.81.

Aztec Sculpture

Pages 64-7 Stone 'chacmool' figure, *c*.AD 1400-1500. Such figures were a characteristic feature of Toltec temple sculpture (*c*.AD 1000-1200). This Aztec-period example has the typical form with the reclining figure supporting an offering vessel, but is smaller than is typical of Toltec and Maya-Toltec 'chacmool' figures. Length 42 cm. 1825.12-10 (Bullock Collection).

Page 67 (*Below*) Henry Moore's *Memorial Figure*, 1945-6, Hornton stone. Dartington Hall, Totnes, Devon.

Pages 68, 71-2 Aztec stone figure of a man, *c*.AD 1400-1500, possibly representing the god Xochipilli, god of flowers, pleasure and feasting. Height 54 cm. 1825.12-10 (Bullock Collection).

Pages 69-70 Aztec stone figure, *c*.AD 1400-1500, probably representing the death god Mictlantecuhtli, who dwelt in the underworld, the region of death. Height 59 cm. 1849.6-29.2 (Wetherell Collection).

Page 73 (*Above*) Henry Moore's *Draped Seated Woman*, 1957-8, bronze. Hebrew University, Jerusalem. (*Below*) see pp.34-5.

Page 74 Aztec stone rattlesnake, *c*.AD 1400-1500. This powerful carving, with fangs, rattle and other details clearly shown, is typical of the best Aztec sculpture. The underside is also carved and painted with rows of red spots on the segments of the body. The function of such carvings is not known, nor how they were displayed, since it is evident that the underside was meant to be seen. Serpent carvings like this one were associated with the cult of *Xiucoatl* or 'Fire Snake'. Height 35 cm. 1849.6-29.1 (Wetherell Collection).

Page 75 Stone mask of the god Xipe Totec, Aztec, *c*.AD 1400-1500. The god Xipe Totec, 'Our Lord, the Flayed One', was a god of Springtime and planting. In the ceremonies devoted to this deity priests would wear the flayed skin of a sacrificial victim. The facial part of such a skin is clearly represented here. In other sculptures of the same subject, the face of the priest is visible so that, for example, the mouth of the wearer shows through, symbolising the new vegetation which replaces the old. 1956.AmX.6 (Christy Collection).

Oceanic Sculpture

Pages 76-9 Stone statue of Hoa-Haka-Nana-Ia ('Breaking-waves') from Easter Island, collected during the visit of HMS *Topaze* in 1868. The figure was presented by the Lords of the Admiralty to Queen Victoria, who gave it to the British Museum in 1869. Height 264 cm.

Pages 80-1 Painted wood carving commemorating the dead, from New Ireland, Papua New Guinea. Height 144 cm. Q73 Oc.9.

Page 81 (*Left*) Henry Moore's *Internal-External Forms*, 1952-3, bronze. Kunsthalle, Hamburg.

Pages 82-5 Wood image, probably representing A'a, the principal deity of Rurutu, Austral Islands. The detachable back covers the cavity in the body, into which smaller images were originally placed. Height 117 cm. LMS 19.

Pages 86-7 Wood figure of a god, perhaps Tangaroa, the sea god and creator, from Rarotonga, Cook Islands. Height 69 cm. LMS 169.

Page 88 (*Bottom left*) Page 90 from Henry Moore's Notebook No.3, 1922-4. (Photo by courtesy of the Henry Moore Foundation)

Pages 88-9 Wood image of a deity from Hawaii. Length 67 cm. 1657.

Page 90 Wood figure from the Karawari River, East Sepik Province, Papua New Guinea. Height 119 cm. 1976 Oc.15.

Page 91 Wood carving representing a war and hunting spirit from the Karawari River, East Sepik Province, Papua New Guinea. Height 238 cm. 1976 Oc.13.

African Sculpture

Pages 92–3 see p.97

Pages 94–5 Wood male and female figures, probably from the district of Yambio close to Sudan's border with Zaire. This style of carving seems to have emerged here in the late nineteenth century but is unrelated to other forms of Azande work. It might be that this style is the work of itinerant carvers attracted to one of the centres of the expansionist Azande princedoms. Heights 80 cm, 52 cm. 1949.Af46.522,523.

Page 96 Wood double-headed dog from Bakongo, Zaire, regarded as a repository of good or evil influences that might be manipulated by driving nails into the body of the object. Length 61 cm. 1905.5-26.6.

Page 97 Wood figure from Bakongo, Zaire, possessing the same ambiguous properties as that above (page 96) and activated in the same way. Height 110 cm. 1905.5-25.3.

Pages 98–9 Wood figure representing a female ancestor, from Baluba, Zaire. Height 46 cm. 1910.441.

Pages 100–2 Wood caryatid in the distinctive style developed around the turn of the century in the vicinity of Buli, a village in Eastern Zaire. Height 52 cm. 1905.6-13.1.

Page 101 (*Bottom left*) Page 126 from Henry Moore's Notebook No.3 (detail), 1922–4. (Photo by courtesy of the Henry Moore Foundation)

Page 103 Wood headrest from Baluba, Zaire. The two figures are thought to be wrestlers, and have the cascading coiffure of the Shankadi subtribe. Height 19 cm. 1949.Af46.481.

Pages 104–5 Wood Bajokwe figure representing Chibinda Ilunga, an early hunter chief and culture hero. Height 34 cm. 1969.Af9.5.

Pages 106–7 Wood helmet mask, said to represent a female spirit, from Baga, Guinee. 1957.Af7.1.

Pages 108–9 Bronze head of a Queen Mother, from Benin, Nigeria, probably dating to the early sixteenth century. Height 39 cm. 1897.10-11.1.

American and Caribbean Sculpture

Pages 110–11 see pp.118–19

Pages 112–13 Standing wood figure of a man from Taino, Jamaica, probably pre-Hispanic. This figure is one of a group of three carvings 'Found in June, 1792 in a natural cave near the summit of a mountain called Spots in Carphenters [sic] Mountain in the parish of Vere, by a surveyor in measuring the land'. Few wood sculptures survive from the pre-Hispanic period, and nothing is known of the use or meaning of this group, although they probably represent deities and had a ceremonial function. Height 103 cm. Q77 Am3.

Page 114 (*Above*) Page 90 from Henry Moore's Notebook No.3, 1922–4. (Photo by courtesy of the Henry Moore Foundation)

Pages 114–15 Wood stool or *duho* in the form of a human figure, from Taino, Jamaica, probably pre-Hispanic. Of the rare wood carvings which survive from the Caribbean region, the *duho* is the most common type, although this example is of rather unusual form, the sculptor having clearly taken advantage of the shape of the piece of wood from which it was made. Length 72 cm. 9753.

Pages 116–17 Wood standing figure of a man with the head of a bird, probably representing a *zemi*, a spirit or deity. From Taino, Jamaica, probably pre-Hispanic. Height 88 cm. Q77 Am2.

Page 117 (*Right*) Henry Moore's *Upright Motive*, 1955–6, bronze. Israel Museum, Jerusalem.

Pages 118–19 Nootkan alderwood bowl from British Columbia with two human figures as handles. Length 22 cm. Am5 1.

Pages 120–1 Nootkan wood figure of a mother and child, from Vancouver Island, British Columbia. Height 27·5 cm. NWC 64.

Pages 122–3 Nootkan wood figure of a mother and child, from Vancouver Island, British Columbia. Height 38 cm. NWC 66.

Page 124 Henry Moore's *Family Group*, 1948–9, bronze. The Museum of Modern Art, New York.

Page 125 (*Left*) Page 103 from Henry Moore's Notebook No.3 (detail), 1922–4. (*Right*) Nootkan wood figure of a mother and child. Height 16 cm. NWC 62.